Our Solemn Stars

Victoria Stevens

BookLeaf Publishing

India | USA | UK

Presentation by *BookLeaf Publishing*

Web: www.bookleafpub.com

E-mail: info@bookleafpub.com

ISBN: 9789363310308

First edition 2024

*To the stars who guide me through the darkest
parts of my life. Thank you.*

Our Solemn Stars

The world is so dark,
we've all grown to know.
When even the brightest parts
feel colder than the snow.

A sky so dark
can grow so bright.
Revealing pieces of ourselves
hidden from sight.

There's nothing to fear
for as you grow,
within the shadows
stars begin to glow.

For every memory,
you'll reach a new height.
Fleeting moments
will chase away the night.

Whether dearest friend
or mighty foe,
every face we meet
will cause stars to show.

We'll struggle through life,
and amidst our fight.
It'll shape who we are,
we'll discover our might.

A hollow universe
will be full of woe.
A starry sky
is what we sow.

Wish

"Blow out the candles!"
And so I did.
"Make a wish!"
And so I did.

Every candle.
Every dandelion.
Every star.

Like a broken record,
the words repeat in my head.
A mantra I have begun to need.

I wish,
I wish,
I wish for hope.

I wish, I do, for hope itself.

How are you really?

I'm fine.

Other than staying up 'til six a.m.
When stories filled my mind,
and worries kept my eyes wide.

I'm fine.

Other than sudden bursts of crying.
Feeling completely numb
until tears suddenly stung.

I'm fine.

Other than everything feeling like a lie.
I don't know who I am
and the answer frightens me.

I'm fine.

Other than walking like spirit untied.
I feel like a ghost in disguise,
a fractured reflection of my soul in time.

How am I?
How am I really?

I'm fine.

I'm fine.

3 a.m.

I stare at my phone.
Tears sting my eyes,
I've been afraid to cry.

I'm texting my closest friend.
Telling them things
that'd be better left unsaid.

My heart's screaming.
My brain can't prevent
my soul from bleeding.

I'm unlearning everything
I've taught myself.
My truest self I've been in eons.

Worry

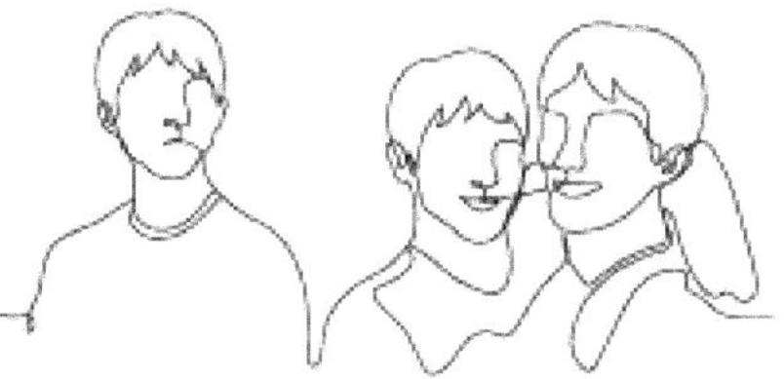

"You look worried."

"Well, how could I not be?
When someone so tall
looks ready to fall,
how could I not be?"

"You shouldn't be worried."

"How could I not?
When someone so strong
is feeling so wrong,
how could I not?"

"Just escape from your thoughts."

"Look at them there,
Their darkening stare.
How can I escape,
When they're in a place
most would not dare.
How are you not scared?"

"Scared of what?
Their poisoning thoughts?
They have their thoughts,
I have my own.
So, scared of what?
Of what I can't care?"

"They are your friend,
that's what you said.
Why are you not scared?
Why do you not care?"

"Why should I?
My problems are mine!
They could not care!
They wouldn't be scared!"

"They are them.
You are you.
Their choices are theirs.
Yours define you."

"My choices are mine.
Who cares what they define?
I am not scared.
I do not care."

"They have poisonous thoughts.
They can't escape,
they can't outrun,
their toxic mental waste."

"So, they're feeling wrong?
As you said, they are strong.
Why should I care
when I know they can bear?
They stand so tall.
They can catch
themselves if they fall.
Why should I be scared?"

"Why would you not be?"

"Because then I have to care.
If I care,
and they still fall…
Why should I care?"

"You almost sound worried."

"I shouldn't be worried."

"You seem lost in your head."

"I can't escape from my dread.
These thoughts are scary."

"Worry is caring."

"Worry is scary."

Haunting

I can see ghosts.

I can see them on sidewalks,
in restaurants, and parks.

I can see them in hotels,
libraries, and coffee shops.

I can see them in theatres,
classrooms, and piers.

I can see them in airports,
museums, and even here.

Ghosts exist among the living.

I can hear their heartbeats,
I see them breathe.

I know they bleed,
I've seen them scrape their knees.

I hear their whispers,
and I hear their screams.

I hold their hands in mine,
make the invisible feel seen.

Ghosts are still alive.

Some of them are friends,
others are strangers.

Some of them laugh,
others feel empty.

Some of them are vibrant,
others fade away.

Some of them leave,
others haunt this plane.

The Boy Half Alive

Hiding in the shadows
afraid to be seen.

Shaking in the cold,
begging for heat.

Hollow eyes
stare up at the sky.

Counting the stars,
he can barely see five.

Listening to his pulse,
unaware if it still beats.

Counting his breaths,
unsure if he still needs to breathe.

The snow still crunches
beneath his feet.

And the cold air
brings color to his cheeks.

He knows he's alive,
he knows he's not.

He knows he's dead,
he knows he's not.

Like a ghost
fading from the light.

Like a ghost,
fading from life.

Blue

I'm drowning
        and drowning
                drowning in blue

I'm sick of the color
        it feels overused

I used to see gold
        it has faded away

I wanted it back
        for the blue to change shade

I wanted it
        I wanted it
                I wanted it so bad

If I can't reach gold,
        I'll welcome black
                like an old friend
                        who finally came back

Shattered

I believe we are all made of glass.

I do not mean we are fragile.
I do not mean we are all broken.

I mean we can shatter.
I mean we can be fixed.

I mean that the broken become sharper.
I mean the broken become smarter.

I mean we cannot be fixed with scotch tape.
I mean we cannot be fixed with glue.

I mean the broken lines are visible.
I mean the scars do not leave.

I mean we are beautiful.
I mean we shine in the light.

I mean we are durable.
I mean we survive our fights.

I mean we are strong.

I mean we can break.

I mean we can heal.

I mean we will not shake.

I mean we will make it.

I mean we will shine.

I mean it.

No matter how broken,
we will all thrive.

Traitor

I trusted you.
I. Trusted. You.

They say write
what you know.

I'll tell you
what I know.

I know you
betrayed me.

After everything.
Everything.

And do you know
what's worse?

Is that I know you,
so, I know why.

I know why
you betrayed me.

I know how
it all fell apart.

And honestly,
I hate you for it.

And I hate me too.
Traitor.

Revenge

I have felt betrayal's blade.

The scars run deeper than I'll say.

My bleeding soul screams in pain.

Siphoning my life away.

Revenge is cold

But I still burn.

Agony as hellfire turns.

Scars given without shame.

Made her look me in the face.

A promise of destruction reigns.

Echoed in my pain-filled rage.

Ire within my bloodstained cage.

Only poison in my veins.

Taunted by my broken chains.

You will rue the day you learned my name.

The Grave

You scream your vile lies into the wind.
You pray for my downfall.
I stand at your level,
meeting your eyes.

I listen as every untruthful word
entangles into the web you've created.
I watch as you bury yourself
in the grave you dug for me.

Your lies will be plastered across your
tombstone.

Karma's Watching

I will watch you fall.

I will watch you fail.

I will not laugh.

I will not smile.

I will not feel triumph.

For no matter how broken

our bond has become,

there was a time

I would've fought at your side.

I would've fallen with you.

You tried to ruin my life.

Blame me as you wish,

but I will watch.

I will watch you fall.

I will watch you fail.

I will not laugh.

I will not smile.

I will not feel triumph.

But I will feel alright.

Maze

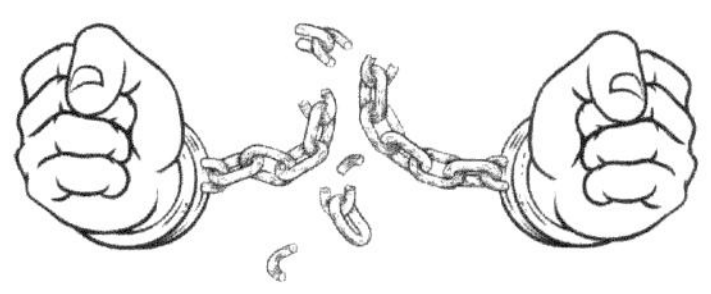

Running until I can barely breathe.
Sticks and stones scrape my feet.
A trail of blood follows me,
the grass turns red as I sneak.

The walls stand high,
I can barely see the sky.
The word "lost" fills my head,
quick as the tears in my eyes.

Left, left,
right, right.
Wrong way, again.
Just another dead end.

As I start to lose fight,
it shines in the light.
The end is in sight,
standing with might.

The golden gate marks the end of the line.
Vines are tangled along the sides.
Chains keep it locked tight
keeping me from the freedom I desire.

My fist hits the lock.
Again, again, again, and again.
The curses I mutter
get lost in the wind.

I see the fields on the other side.
The sea of wheat marks the peace.
I crave an escape, the open skies.
"Please, please, please," I plead.

The gates won't move,
No matter how hard I try.
They won't budge,
they won't give way.

My desperate pleas
only echo in my mind.
No one else around
to hear my sorrowful cries.

No escape.
No matter how hard I try.

Gravedigger

In the grave that I dug for myself,
I lay quieter than those I surround.
Dirt falls on my face, gentle and strong.
I hear the shovel sing its solemn song.

Remind me of my shortcomings.
Remind me of my wrongs.
Show me how my story ends,
before we reread chapter one.

Always had one foot on the ground,
one foot in the grave.
Ready for the changing winds
to decide my eternal fate.

The regret that I wield
will be the reason I lay in this field.
As the end grows near, I refuse to show fear.
My choices are what brought me here.

I carved my own tombstone.
The shallow words read,
"Here lies she, the girl who could not be
all that they wish to see."

Ode to the Stranger

I see you on the street,
Our eyes accidentally meet.
I don't mean to stare,
but I recognized you there.

I didn't smile,
not meaning to be rude.
I was just a little stunned,
But you were too.

You're surrounded by your friends,
and me around mine.
I don't recognize their faces,
you barely recognize mine.

I wanted to ask you
how you've been,
how you are,
do you recognize me?

Seeing you brings back memories,
forgotten pieces of me.
What's with the fake smile?
Why's mine the same?

Do you remember me?
All we've done.
All we've seen.
We could drown in our memories.

Hours seemed to pass
as our gazes crossed paths.
But we never stopped,
didn't even hesitate.

They ask if I know you.
I watch how you move,
how you talk and laugh.
I finally look away, the end of that.

Shaking my head,
moving on once again.
We were friends once,
but we're strangers in the end.

I Remember, I Miss, I Wish

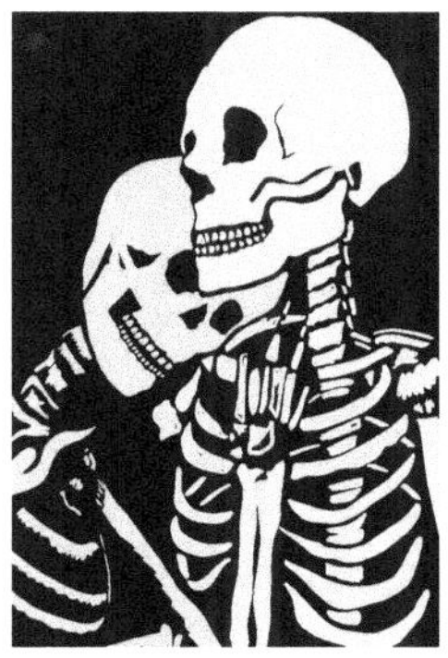

I often forget
what the thought of you
does to my mind.

You're not even here
but your name makes
the world so much brighter.
Compared to others
who have come and gone,
you shine like the sunlight hitting snow.

Your name leaves
a sweet taste on my tongue,
reminding me of the nights
we spent smiling bright.
Those moments felt
like a suspension in time,
reality melting away from life.

I look back
on memories of you
with a bittersweet smile,
desiring more.

I miss you.

Next Time

Maybe next time
I'll say it.

Maybe next time
you'll know.

Maybe next time
you'll say it.

Maybe next time
I'll know.

Maybe next time
won't happen.

Maybe next time
doesn't exist.

Maybe next time
I shouldn't wait so long.

Maybe next time
I won't be left wondering.

Maybe next time
I'll know there's a next time.

Missing Piece

How sad it would be
to spend eternity searching
for a missing piece?

A soulmate,
they'll call it.
Your "other half".

Then what am I now?
A pathetic excuse
of what I'm meant to be?

It's an innocent myth
that seeks to fracture
my sense of being.

Why would I seek
for my "missing piece"
when I have yet to lose anything?

I don't even get a century.
Why waste the little time I'll be,
living for someone unseen?

I am not
what I could be.
But nothing is missing.

Undiscovered?
Yes.
Not unobtained.

I'll live for me.
I'll live my life.
I'll pave my path.

I'll pave it for me,
not for someone
I have yet to meet.

I am not without love,
without hope, or dreams.
I do crave the one unseen.

But I'll pave my path.
Who knows where it leads?
Maybe, one day I will see.

I will not love
"my missing piece".
I'll love all they will be.

I'll love their path
and they'll love mine.
Maybe, paths will one day align.

For now,
I'll do me.
And I will be.

I will not
live for my
"missing piece".

Ice Cream

The annoying glow of the fluorescent lights.
The bitter taste of the ice cream I kind of dislike.

Ire-filled glares of the minimum wage workers.
And the sickening smell of tons of sugar.

Somewhere I love with all my being.

In face of such contradictions,
I dance the line like a tightrope circus.

Something I love, something I loathe.
Not quite a home away from home.

A place I'll cherish as the years pass by.

After some of the best and worst
days of my untried life.

The purest moments I've been gifted
within the storms of days so vicious.

The friendships I'll never regret making.

The memories I'll dream of recreating.

Within the nightmares, I found some peace.

With dearest friends and vanilla ice cream.

As the Stars Fade...

I've grown used to the light.
The vibrance in night.

Stars guide my way,
through treacherous sights.

I've relied on them well
when the world feels like hell.

"Thank you," I say.
Something I've been meaning to tell.

One day, the memories will fade.
It's a truth I often evade.

I know your echo will stay,
even if it hides in the shade.

I love you all.

I forever will.

In a life full of darkness,
you light up my world.

Scripted

I followed the script.
The perfect play.
Word for word,
day by day.

I followed the script.
Becoming the character,
You asked me to play.
One you wanted me to portray.

I followed the script.
Obeyed your every wish.
Call me a genie.
See these chains on my wrist?

I followed your script.
Your stupid little play.
These words aren't mine.
Wasting my life away.

To Love

To love what is loved
is a curse to rot.

To love what is loved
by those who say you cannot.

To love what is loved,
oh, how it hurts!

To love what is loved
when it is not yours.

Today

I sat beside you today.

You haven't changed.
You stand a little taller.
You stand a little stronger.
But you're still the same.

I sat beside you today.

You told a joke.
You made me laugh.
I forgot what it was like,
Listening to the words you crack.

I sat beside you today.

You remembered.
What I knew,
what we do.
You remembered me.

I sat beside you today.

Can I sit beside you tomorrow?

Know

You don't know.
At least, I hope.

She's known for years.
He's known for months.
She's known for weeks.
He's known for days.

I've known for minutes.

All of that's fine
As long as you don't.

You don't know.

Forgetting

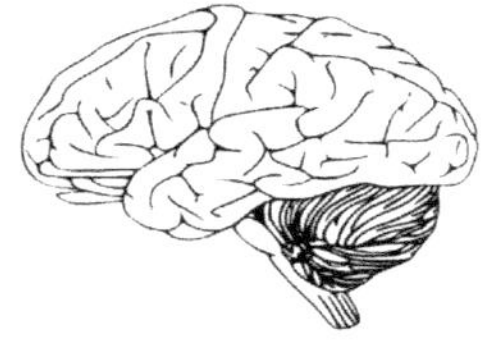

Forgetting
is a drug I crave.
The allure of pain
leaving one's brain.

Forget the past.
Forget the tears.
Forget the heartache.
Forget.

If you forget the pain,
It'll all go away,
right?

Home

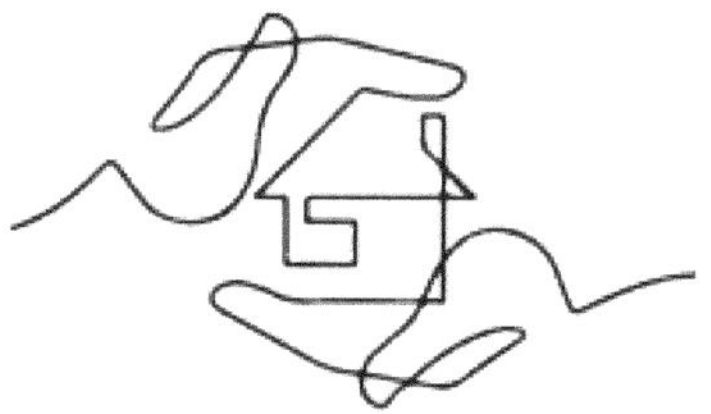

I want to go home.
A phrase we all know.
What is your home?
An answer not easily shown.

A house?
A family?
A close friend?
A distant memory?

I remember missing school,
burning up, chills up my spine.
As I lay in my bed,
incoherent words flew off my tongue.
I want to go home.

I remember staring at a test.
The clock had barely hit eight,
my eyelids gave me a workout
as I was fighting to stay awake.
I want to go home.

I remember sitting alone at lunch.
A notebook in my lap,
millions of words within my grasp.
Nonexistent motivation.
I want to go home.

I remember last night.
The glowing clock mocked me.
Insomnia, my old friend,
came for a visit yet again.
I want to go home.

What is your home?
I still don't know.

My house?
My family?
My close friend?
My distant memory?

Maybe it's what
I need it to be,
A place that provides
the comfort I need.

All I know?
I want to go home.

"Grow Up," They Said

When you say goodbye to your childhood,
of what are you truly letting go?
You tell yourself,
"I'm growing up, so what?
Just a number going up."

But something inside you,
dies before you'll ever know.
Your hopes, your dreams,
they decide it's time to go.
Or were you the first
to leave them behind?
That's something I still don't know.

"Grow up," they said.
"It's wonderful," they said.
What's so wonderful on this side of the line?
I see pain wherever I go,
everyone's hearts are filled with sorrow.

You find out more
because they said you could.
You find out more
because they said you should.
You find out more
because they no longer care to hide the truth.
Where is the wonderful world I was promised?

"Grow up," they said.
I should've said, "no."

Hope

I hold to the hope
that one day,
somewhere down the line,
I won't have to ask
if you'll be there.

Because
all I'll have to do
is turn my head
and see you
holding my hand.

Alive

I am happy to know
I loved someone so deeply.

No matter how brief,
I loved something.

And that means I'm alive.

It means my heart still beats.

Unexpected

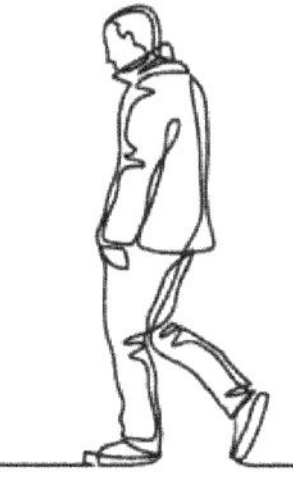

Of course,
I had been wishing
for someone to love,
but I never thought
I'd find it with you.

For years,
your name echoed
in the background of my life,
never present but never gone.
You were nothing more
than a passing wind,
I'm sure I was even less.

Your name has become something I crave.
You have become something I crave.
Something I desire.

You were unexpected.

I expect to see you again tomorrow.

Two Weeks

In a perfect world,
I'd know how I feel.
In a perfect world,
I'd know what you think.

Instead, I sit in the dark,
alone with my thoughts.
Your name echoes in my mind,
interrupting thoughts far from sight.

I do not know how I feel,
despite the words I write.
I'm lost, I'm confused,
you've thrown me for a loop.

You were unexpected.
You were nearly unwarranted.
You entered my life,
stumbling in without remorse.

I keep asking myself,
how did it happen?
How did you grow on me
in such a small amount of time?

To My Big Sister

To the girl who taught me to draw the sun.
The swirls on the page
are forever embedded in my memory.

To the girl who helped me learn to ride a bike.
Until we steered headfirst
into the side mirror of my brother's truck.

To the girl who grew up in the same house as
me.
We fought and bickered endlessly.
I don't regret any memories.

To my big sister.
The one I idolized
pretty much all my life.

To my big sister.
Thank you.
I love you.

Stormchaser

Oh, storm chaser,
eyes on the sky.
When lightning strikes
you'll never shy.

Oh, storm chaser,
head in the clouds.
You embrace the wind,
getting carried with the crowd.

Oh, storm chaser
with thy silver tongue.
I trust not
the songs you've sung.

Oh, storm chaser,
heart so wrong.
What drove you
to chase such harm?

Oh, storm chaser,
conscience gone.
I resent the
storm you brought on.

Giving Up

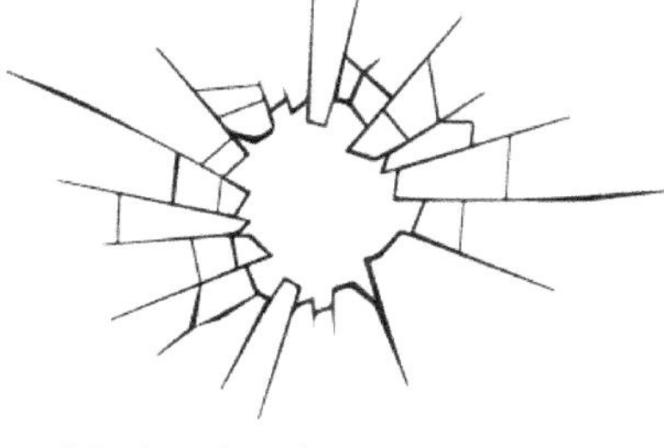

Stab me with the shards
of my broken hopes and dreams.

Maybe their remnants
will remind my heart to beat.

Or maybe I'll just bleed.
Both are fine with me.

The Flower

There's a flower in my garden
it stands taller than the best.
The roots run deeper
than the rest.

The flower stands
among the weeds,
thinking it is
merely a leaf.

Its golden petals
shine so bright,
I wonder how it
doesn't see its own light.

When the winter comes,
it may fade.
But I know it will
come back one day.

When the weeds
tear at the concrete,
I trust the flower
will not hurt me.

So, I say thank you to the flower
and all it's given me.
The only time I didn't
have to fight to be seen.

Silence

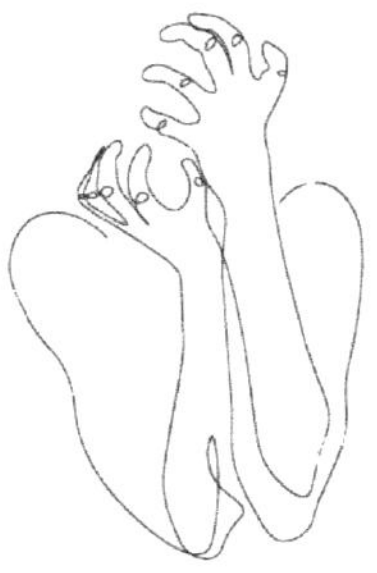

The silence
in between our screams
are more terrifying
than the words we bleed.

Souls mimic
a banshee's plea.
When the screaming stops,
peaceful it seems.

That's when my heart
finds the means.
Our mouths stop moving
the fog starts clearing.

I'll see you for more
than what you seem.
I'm sorry, my friend.
Blind I may be.

Black Sheep

Dearest Black Sheep,
I see your fleece.
Standing out
among the snow-white sleeves.

Dearest black sheep,
I hear your pleas.
Your darkened heart
begs for relief.

Dearest black sheep,
I can see.
The paint stains
you hide beneath.

Dearest black sheep,
you're like the rest.
Snow-white fleece
hidden within your chest.

Dearest black sheep,
it's alright.
Sometimes we need to stand out
before we can accept the inside.

Forgiveness

To forgive
is my Achilles heel.
I need to stop,
it's so cruel.

Let in the fox,
and it steals the eggs.
The other hens
hate their gaze.

Despite the betrayal,
I accept them again.
Letting them back in,
without hesitation.

A simple sorry,
sometimes less.
I often end up apologizing
over what they did to me.

They call me strong
until they see.
They use me
until I'm weak.

And I'll still say sorry
again and again
for not giving
all of me to them.

I'm sorry.
But not to them.
Not again.
I'm sorry to me.

I'm sorry, my forgiveness is earned so easily.

Colorful

My friend and I once played a game.

What color is our personality?

We rattled off our friends' given labels.

Yellow, blue, purple, and pink.

I don't remember theirs; I think it was green.

I remember what they labelled me.

Grey.

I was grey.

I could've taken offense, but I think they were right.

I agreed.

To think I was so drained of color…

The very absence of it represented me.

My friends and I played a game.

What color is our personality?

Never have I been prouder to be considered red.

Cravings

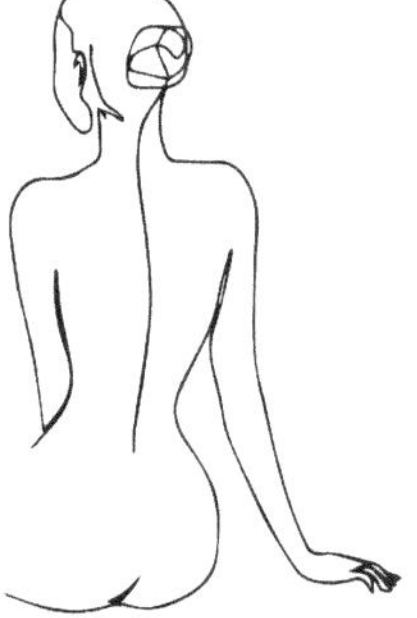

How can I crave
the name of someone
I've never met?

Syllables I've yet to utter
plague my heart
with relentless banter.

I desire to
unscramble the letters that
have yet to invade my brain.

How can I
miss something
I have not lost?

How can I
miss something
I'll probably never gain?

To Live

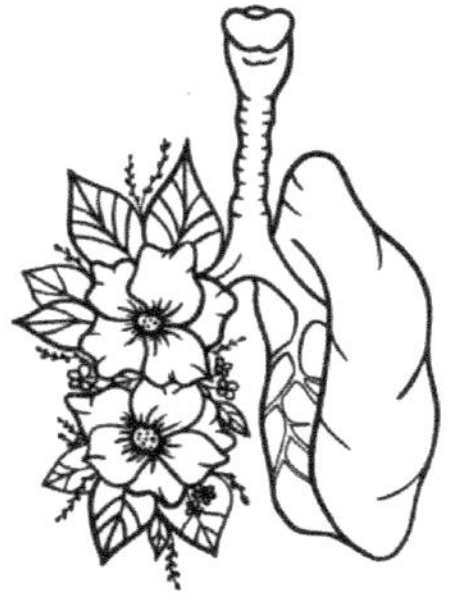

The first time I saw death,
I was around seven years old.

A funeral for a woman
for whom respect I still hold.

I was told a short phrase,
It stuck with me so.

There is a difference
between living and surviving.

The idea terrified me,
I was just a kid.

As I grew old,
I understood what they meant.

I learned that surviving
is just not enough.

Life is not worth it
If you can't truly live.

Scars

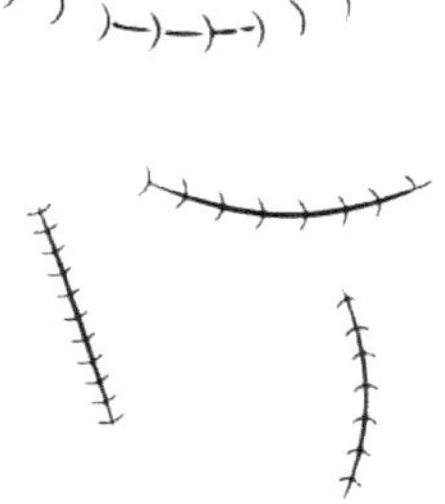

I have scars on my hands.
Given to me by oil-popping
and ice skate slicing.

I have scars on my arms.
Caused by hot pans
and glue guns.

I have scars on my legs.
Gifted to me by pets
and by friends.

I have a scar on my head.
Earned it as a kid
by protecting a friend.

My scars hold memories.
A permanent reminder
of those I left behind.

Little pieces of them
forever embedded
deep in my skin.

The white strike across my finger
reminds me of a friend
I've long outgrown.

I have a scar on my shin,
It came from retaliation.
My bad I guess.

I have a scar on my thigh.
I love that dog,
despite her claws.

I treasure my scars.
They are mine.
They are me.

I am living proof
of those I've passed by.

To My Dad,

Whether you noticed or not,
I loved reading your poems as a kid.
I remember when you were on trips,
I'd steal the books from under your bed.

I'm more like you than I often believe.
An echo of the man who raised me.
The fleeting moments I notice,
I just hope you're proud of me.

I love you, dad.
One day you'll see,
I'll be everything and more
of what you hope I will be.

We Were Never in Love

We were never in love.

You loved me; you did.
You told me,
but not back then.

We were never in love.

I loved you; I did.
I told you,
but not back then.

We were never in love.

The words that burned,
never spilled from our lungs.
Forever left unsaid.

We loved.

We were never in love.

Again

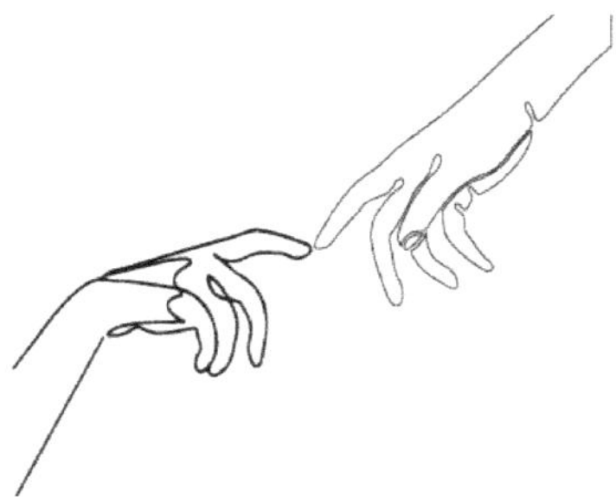

If you gave me the chance, I'd take it.

I've thought about it a lot.

This wouldn't be a sudden decision.

It's gone wrong once.

Everyone says it's a lost cause.

Our friends would have thoughts.

They'd try to convince me otherwise.

It might be a bad idea.

I'd say yes anyways.

I want to hold your hand in mine again.

I want to see your hesitant smile again.

I want you to look at me again.

I'd say yes.

I'd say yes if you asked me again.

Myself

I want to say I lost myself because of you.

It'd be a lie.

I lost myself long before you walked in.

But…

I only let you stay because I was lost.

And yet…

I lost more of myself because I let you stick around.

Clay

i am made of clay
remade
by those who detested my shape

warped and formed
criticized
under the cruelest gaze

covered in marks
preserved
the gentle prints of harsh hands

we are all made of clay
destroying
each other day by day

Smile

I once relearned to smile.
I promise it's not fun.
It's certainly not simple,
but it's a memory I love.

My smile's not the prettiest
but it is bright.
My pictures are horrendous,
that wasn't the point.

I can smile now,
a simple growth.
A single change,
a new view of the world.

Heavy

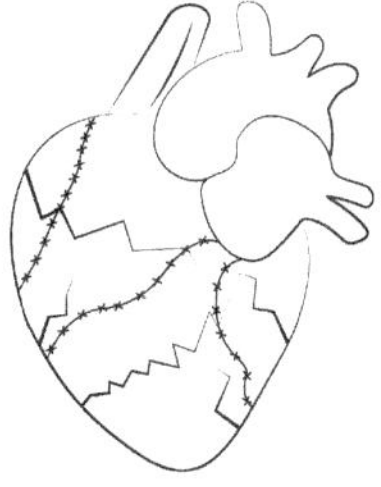

I never understood
a "heavy heart".
The expression escaped me
the phrase seemed silly.

But now I sit here,
my heart sinking.
It feels heavy
as tears are stinging.

Perception

It's odd how happiness is perceived.

I could say something common,
like how hard it is to reach.

While true, it's not what I mean.

I have spent years not smiling,
now I smile constantly.

I am happier now; I see it as a good thing.

Over the years, I've seen a shift.
The way people see me has kind of flipped.

How can a smile change their view so
drastically?

I used to be called smart,
now they mostly say I'm naïve.

I've paid my dues, and then I grew.

My opinion is no longer valued,
even if the words are the same.

Apparently thinking out loud is something fools
do.

Maybe my voice is higher,
maybe it's just a cliché.

Maybe being happy isn't enough in their eyes.

I used to be scary,
intimidating, and strong.

I can see why a smile shatters that mold.

Despite all that's happened,
I don't think I've changed much inside.

I'm loyal and strong, I swear I stayed kind.

Nothing's changed much inside.
But I'm a lot happier where I preside.

I haven't changed, so why have their eyes?

My happiness should not be treated as a
disguise.

Bittersweet

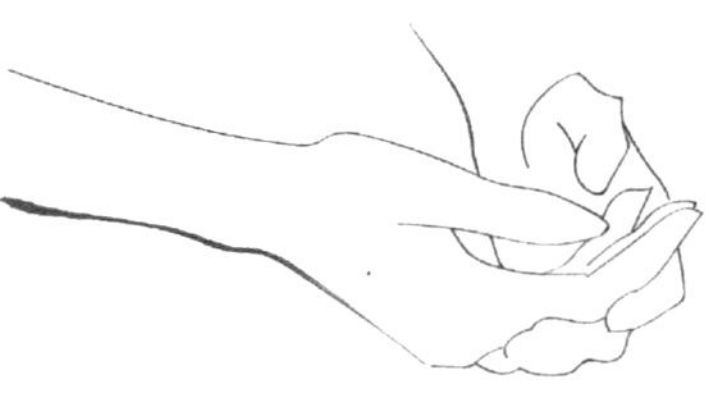

Ice cream doesn't taste as good anymore.

It's bittersweet.

It's cold.

I don't think I'll go again, not with them.

They're bittersweet.

They're cold,

I don't love ice cream anymore.

Love

People love you.

Someone loves you.

Never doubt that.

Your parents.

Your siblings.

Your friends.

Your coworkers.

Your classmates.

Someone.

Someone loves your smile.

Someone loves your hugs.

Someone loves your habits.

Someone loves your words.

Someone loves you.

You are loved.

Both

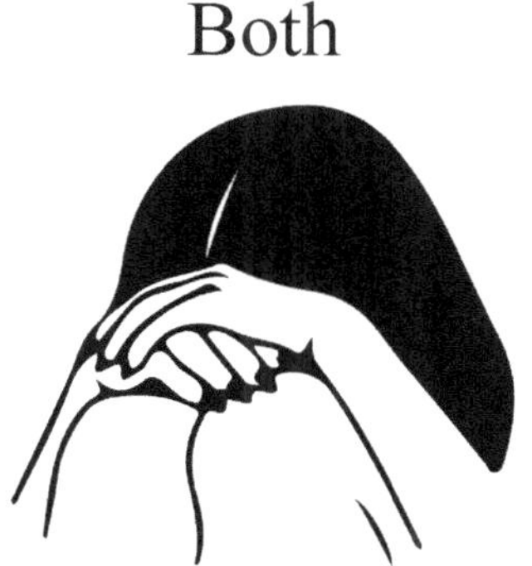

To some,
I'm not enough.

To some,
I'm too much.

How can I be both?
Can someone be both?

Something I've noticed…

During my darkest days
I'm never enough.

During my brightest,
I'm way too much.

Those who come during the darkest,
can't stand me when I glow.

They leave.

Those who come during my brightest,
won't be there when the darkness hits.

They leave.

A constant cycle.
And then I'm alone.

I can't be both.

How Far

You stand above us all
atop the corpses of the fallen.

A pearly-white smile
built of polished canines.

Admired like
a gold-plated gun.

You silence the ones
that've gone too far.

How far would you go
to stay on the pedestal you've conquered.

Coffin

Said I'd make it out alive.
But I think I lied.
I'm losing in the war I've tried.

Six feet below the world I've loathed.
I told myself I was ready to go,
yet I fight to hold the ones I know.

I said that I was fine as they nailed the lid on.
Giving up my soul, yet desiring to live.
How long ago was the coffin built?

I'm not ready to go.
I know, darling.
My dying words written in stone.

I'm sorry.

I'm sorry.

The Foundation

I built a home
of sticks and twine.

Fragile and small,
but it protected my life.

Helpful hands
came from every side.

We built a home
that reached the skies.

Made from clay and stone
it's where we roam.

Walls filled with love,
laughter, and life.

I built a home.
It fell apart.

I built a home.
I lost my heart.

Stories, Legacy, Infamy

Long after we're gone, what will they read?

Will we be heroes, saving lives?

Will we be villains, made of corruption and spite?

Are we the heroes basking in light?

Are we the kings of our so-called holy land?

Are we tomorrow's monuments?

Are we secrets to be buried out of shame?

Icarus

My dearest, Icarus,
rest your wings.

The sun's aurous glow
may be tempting to know.

Do not approach,
I beg thee so.

My dearest, Icarus,
I won't take your hand.

You look beautiful in the sky,
and I wish I could stand.

But flying, my dear,
is not worth what comes next.

With a sun so bright,
the fall is not worth the flight.

Gilded Heart

Oh, lovely girl,
heart of gold.
Your kindness
truly shows.

Oh, lovely girl,
words so sweet.
Poison disguised
as a sugary treat.

Oh, lovely girl,
beautiful face.
A mask so delicate,
like a cold embrace.

Oh, wretched girl,
heart of coal.
Gilded heart
with a rotten core.

Hurt

Run me through
with the blade
forged by bones
of those I refused to forgive.

The guilt hurt more
than the ire ever did.

Avoidance

Avoid me.

Avoid
my gaze,
my face,
my word.

Avoid me.

Avoid
the truth,
the hurt,
the fear.

Avoid me.

Avoid what you did.

Avoid everything.

Population: Not Enough

We live in a world
with over eight billion people.

I remember first learning about
the seven billion people on this planet,
and now there's more?

How ridiculous.

There's eight billion people.

And I still feel alone when the lights go out.

Graphite and Ink

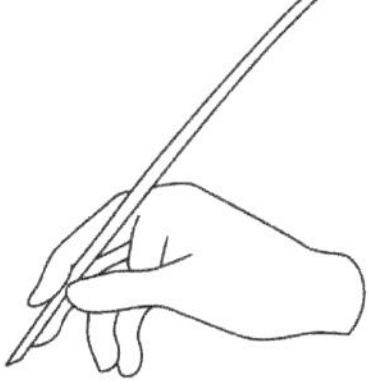

I used to write everything in pencil.

I'd come home from school
with my hands stained grey.

I'd write a million words,
but never found the right thing to say.

I had a teacher.
He told me to write in pen.

Don't be afraid to make mistakes.
Don't erase before you try again.

I write everything in pen.

I have notebooks filled with ink.
Drawings, notes, and things I wish to speak.

My hands stain just as easily, if not more.
But that never stopped me before.

I used to write in pencil,
it begrudgingly became pen.

But now I won't erase before I start again.

Chess

The king is weak.
The queen is powerful.
The bishop is agile.
The rook is strong.
The knight is crafty.

The pawn is small.

The pawn is the start of it all.

Overlooked,
underestimated,
maybe even wrong.

Until it crosses the board,
and it becomes what was lost.

A queen.
A bishop.
A rook.
A knight.

Underestimated
until it finishes its first flight.

Cross the board and what will it be?

I hope it survives long enough to see.

Cruel

Don't be so cruel.

Your mocking words burn my ears,
nearly driving me to tears.

Don't be so cruel.

My broken soul
can't take much more.

Don't be so cruel.

I don't need this.
Please.

Don't be so cruel.

I look to my reflection,
through my tear-filled gaze.

"Don't be so cruel," I say to myself.

"Don't be so cruel to yourself."

Pandora's Box

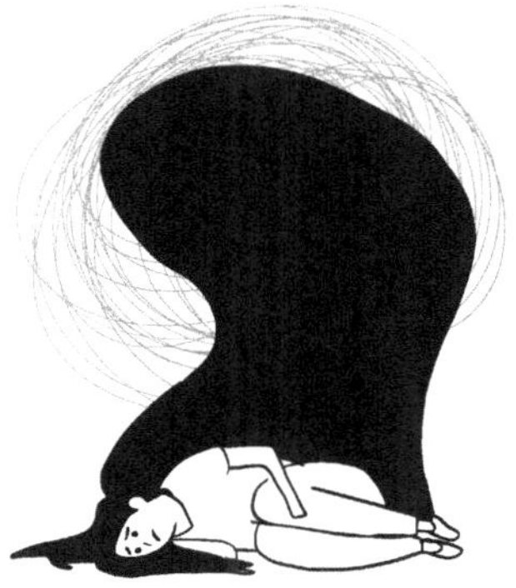

Open it.

Release the darkest
parts of your soul
that stain your heart like coal.

Open it.

Show them the truth.
Make them regret
their callous attitudes.

Open it.

Invite them in.
You'll be free when
the darkness consumes them.

Open it.

Blind their critical gazes.
Infect their poison tongues.
Confine their envious hearts.

Open it.

Show them why you locked it away.

Constellations

My solemn stars
shine so bright.

I watched them dance
on the darkest nights.

I draw the lines in the sky,
connecting them with invisible lines.

They dance together
in eight-count time.

They're drawn together,
much to gravity's ire.

My constellations
shine so bright.

I watch them glow
as I lay below.

I wish I could join
their beautiful show.

Ethereal

My mind is a beautiful place.

Even with my eyes open
I can imagine myself
in a world I create.

My mind is a haunting place.

Every story I write ends the same.
Leaving the characters in so much pain.
It was never over until the storm came.

My mind is a terrifying place.

Its inner workings
are filled with screams.
Painted like a horror movie scene.

My mind is a beautiful place.

My imagination runs rampant.
As strange as it seems,
chaos fulfills my soul's very needs.

Hi mom.

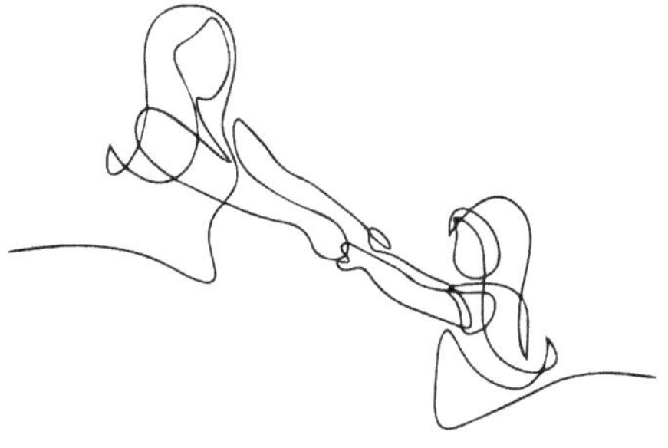

I don't say it enough,
but thank you.

You do a lot,
I know, I promise I do.

You're there when I need it.

You're there if not.

I love you, mom.

I don't say it enough.